Basic Needs

Jean Feldman and Holly Karapetkova

Tune: Head, Shoulders, Knees, and Toes

www.rourkeclassroom.com

air water food shelter

All animals have the
same basic needs.

And that includes you and me!

Little 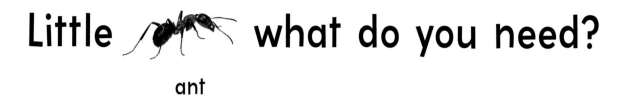 what do you need?

ant

Little 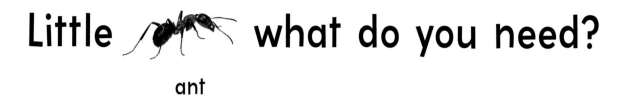 what do you need?

 ,  ,  , and  , too

That's what a little 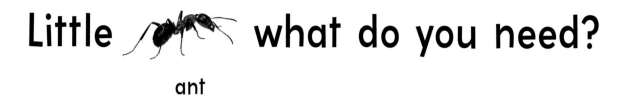 needs.

manatee

what do you need?

what do you need?

 ,  ,  , and  , too

That's what a  needs.

elephant

what do you need?

what do you need?

 ,  ,  , and  , too

That's what an  needs.

 and  what do you need?

boys girls

 and  what do you need?

 ,  ,  , and  , too.

All animals have the same basic needs.